Silly Nomads

Volume 3 Teacher's Guide

Jubilee Bike Race Heroes

Written in collaboration with Progressive Bridges, Inc.
©2017 Mohalland Lewis LLC

© 2017 Mohalland Lewis, LLC
All rights reserved.

© 2016 Document Text
Written in collaboration with
Progressive Bridges, Inc., Naples, FL

Published in the United States by
Mohalland Lewis, LLC

Book Design by Jon Marken
Cover Illustration by Kate Santee

No part of this book may be reproduced, scanned, stored in a retrieval system, or transmitted by any means without the written permission of Mohalland Lewis, LLC.

ISBN 978-0-9990303-2-5

This lesson plan is suitable for use with students in Grades 3-5. All activities are aligned with the ELA Common Core State Standards (CCSS) for Reading, Writing, and Speaking & Listening. Activities can be modified as needed based on specific needs and ability levels within those standards.

Learning Objectives:

1. Identify the characteristics of heroes.
2. Explain and give examples of real and imaginary story events.
3. Compare and contrast characters and settings with one's own life experiences.
4. Engage in using the imagination to help others in need.
5. Utilize and grow literacy skills through story interaction.

This story supports the following beliefs:

- Anyone can be a hero.
- Heroes don't have to have super powers.
- Support, encouragement, and helping each other are all important elements of friendship.
- Doing small acts of kindness are just as important as saving the world.

Note to the Teacher:

Use this lesson plan as a flexible guide to support **Silly Nomads – Volume 3** with a variety of options from which to choose based on your students' interests and ability levels. All activities are aligned with the ELA Common Core State Standards (CCSS) to ensure quality, relevance, and rigor in the academic classroom. Best practice pages for instructional vocabulary activities and read-a-loud strategies are listed on pages 31-33 of this lesson plan document.

A Lesson Guide for Teachers

- **This lesson plan** provides educators with several activity menus that include a range of specific reading skill activities and open-ended questions, aligned with Common Core State Standards (CCSS), enabling students to create meaningful connections to story characters and events as they enhance critical thinking, reading, writing, speaking, and listening skills.

- **This lesson plan** provides educators with cross-curriculum activities to reinforce concepts in social studies, geography, math, science, and the arts, as well as in the area of literacy. Look for specific icons for these connections.

- **This lesson plan** provides educators with a menu of engaging activities for elementary students designed to help them extend their learning by encouraging imaginative and innovative ideas, much like the story characters. Many activities also involve research-related skills designed to appeal to 21st Century learners as they explore a variety of concepts and possible career interests. These activities can be easily modified or adapted for children of many ages, maturity levels, and academic ability levels.

A Home Connection for Students and Parents

- **This lesson plan** provides teachers with learning activities and discussion prompts for students to share with their parents at home to reinforce learning concepts, promote literacy in families, and to provide ways to keep parents connected to the classroom.

 Home Connection Activity

Assessments to Check for Understanding

- **This lesson plan** provides teachers with several assessments to measure student understanding of the story. A Pre and Post Assessment given at the beginning and end of the book provide evidence of concept learning throughout the story. A short 10 question quiz is part of every lesson and measures student comprehension of the part of the book covered for that specific lesson. While most questions are multiple choice or true/false, quizzes do contain a few open-ended responses. A final Reading Comprehension Assessment provides an open-ended response assessment to measure further story comprehension.

Jubilee Bike Race Heroes

Lesson #1   Chapters 1-3   Pages 7-43

Lesson Focus: Suhcrom, Naddih, and their friends go on a bike flying adventure with a bike they've borrowed from Nigel.

Basic Story Vocabulary   (2-5, Reading – Standard 4)

floatation	embankment	propped	forged
electromagnetic	drenched	incline	cylindrical
turbulence	massive	airborne	goggles
g-force	contraptions	swiftly	bloodcurdling
verandas	parish	wheelie	crumpled
escapade	cinder blocks	bawling	comrades

Pre-teach vocabulary to introduce students to new words prior to reading the chapter. Choose an *Instructional Vocabulary Activity* from page 31.

Reading the Text

Silly Nomad books make fun read-aloud experiences for students. Varying these strategies reinforces interaction with text and creates ongoing interest for students. Choose a *Read-Aloud Strategy* from page 32-33 for in-class reading.

Facilitated Discussion Prompts

👓 Have you ever thought about what it would be like to travel to space? Talk with a partner about what it would look like and what you would do. Would you visit another planet or visit the space station? (2-5, Speaking & Listening – Standards 1, 4, & 6)

👀 Watch a short video about space on National Geographic for Kids. Talk with a small group about what you learned from the video and how it is different from what you already knew. (2-5, Speaking & Listening – Standards 1, 2, & 6)

👀 Each of the boys in the story had a special skill. Sterlin could climb anything, Suhcrom was a fast runner, Naddih loved to swim and Rodney could see things that others couldn't. Which of those skills would you rather have? Why? (2-5, Speaking & Listening – Standards 1, 4, & 6)

👀 Based on the title of the book and what you have read so far, make a prediction of what you think will happen in the next reading selection. (2-5, Speaking & Listening – Standards 1, 2, & 6)

👀 Do you think girls are better at riding bikes than boys? Discuss your thoughts with a small group. Explain why or why not. (2-5, Speaking & Listening – Standards 1, 2, & 6)

Reading Comprehension Activities

👀 Create a timeline of words and pictures to retell 5 – 10 events of the story in the order in which they occurred. Add to your story map as you continue to read the book. (2-5, Reading – Standard 2)

👀 Create a t-chart for cause and effect. Find 5-7 events that happened in the story and complete the chart. Younger students can find 3-5 events. (2-5, Reading – Standards 3 & 8)

👀 Use a "Somebody, Wanted, But, So" format to summarize what has happened in the story so far. (2-5, Reading – Standards 4 & 6)

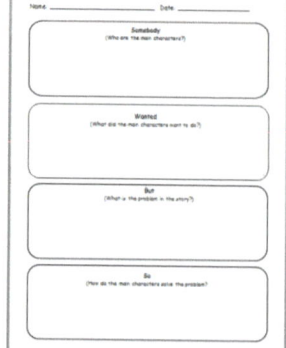

Create a foldable with two columns. On the left side write the word FACTS at the top and on the right side write the word OPINIONS. Find 7-10 facts and opinions in the story and put them in the correct column. Younger students can find 5-7 of each. (2-5, Reading – Standard 4)

Writing Prompts

Imagine that you are taking a trip to Mars on a rocket. Write a story showing how you prepared for the trip and what you saw while you were there. Publish the story and share it with the class. (2-5, Writing – Standards 3, 5, & 6)

Watch an episode of Space Ghost on YouTube. Write an essay comparing and contrasting Space Ghost to your favorite superhero. In your essay, explain why that particular superhero is your favorite. (2-5, Writing – Standard 2, 5 & 6)

Write and illustrate a story with a turtle as the main character. You can make your story funny or to teach a lesson. Share your story with a younger friend or sibling. (2-5, Writing – Standard 3; 2-5, Speaking & Listening – Standard 4)

Rewrite chapter 3 from Muffet's point of view. What did she think of the boys' and Desreen's bike-flying adventure? (2-5, Writing – Standard 3; 2-5, Reading – Standard 6)

Curriculum Connections

Use the internet to research a famous cyclist. Create a digital presentation about the cyclist and his/her life. Share your presentation with the class. (2-5, Writing – Standards 2, 5, 6, & 7; 2-5, Reading – Standards 7 & 9)

Investigate the nutrients that are in turtle meat. Is it good for you? Find a recipe or create your own, using turtle meat. Adjust the recipe so that it will feed 20 people. Write it out on a recipe card and draw a picture of what you think it would look and taste like. Share your recipe with the class. (2-5, Writing – Standard 7)

Jamaica has many different types of landforms – it goes from mountains to the beaches. Research the geography of Jamaica and either draw or print a map of the island. Color in the different types of landforms and where they are on the map. Make sure to create a key for your map. (2-5, Reading – Standard 7)

Turtles live in the water and tortoises live on land. Research some other differences between the two reptiles. Create a poster comparing and contrasting turtles and tortoises. (2-5, Reading – Standards 7 & 9; 2-5, Writing – Standards 2 & 7)

Research & Imagination Activities

 **Imagine Jupiter...**
Imagine that it has become possible for people to live on the planet Jupiter. Research the planet and find out what the conditions are like on the planet. What type of clothes would you need to live on Jupiter? Find a template for a paper doll online or draw one yourself and then create an outfit for your doll. Write a paragraph explaining why you would need each item of clothing. Don't forget to accessorize! (2-5, Reading – Standards 5 & 7)

 **Imagine aliens...**
Imagine that you were an astronaut and you were going on a mission to find life on another planet. You want to take some things with you to give as gifts to the aliens that you might meet so that they can learn about Earth. Think of 5-7 things that you think most represent life on Earth. Either collect the actual objects or find images of the objects. On an index card, write a description of each item and why you think that it would make a good gift for an alien. Use one index card for each item that you have. (2-5, Writing – Standard 2)

 Imagine a cool bike...
Imagine a bicycle with lots of cool gadgets like Nigel's bike in the story. If you could design a bicycle with cool gadgets, how would you design it? What kinds of gadgets would it have and why? Draw a picture of your perfect bike with all its gadgets and explain why you need each item. (2-5, Writing – Standard 2)

  **Imagine turtles...**
Imagine that you were going on a turtle-catching adventure. Who would go with you and what would you need to help you catch turtles? Create a storyboard or a comic strip about your adventure. (2-5, Writing – Standards 3, 5 & 6)

Jubilee Bike Race Heroes - Volume 3

Lesson #1   Home Connection Activities

🏠 Space Ghost had wristbands to send out electromagnetic rays to destroy his enemies. Invent your own superhero. What kinds of powers or tools would he/she have? Construct a paperdoll of your superhero and explain what all his/her tools are for and why they are beneficial.

🏠 Suhcrom and Naddih turned their couch into a space ship. Look around your house. Where would you go on your next imaginary adventure and what could you use as a vehicle for getting there? Take a picture of the item and describe why you choose it and how it would help you get where you were going.

🏠 Jamaica is divided into parishes. Research all the parishes in Jamaica and how they are all different. Create a chart explaining the differences between the parishes.

🏠 Ask a parent to help you learn how to do a wheelie on your bicycle or skateboard. How long did it take you to learn? Keep a journal of what happened and how you felt when you finally learned how to do a wheelie.

WE CONNECTED!

My favorite character in this part of the story was _____

because he/she _____

I liked the part in the story when _____
_____

I circled the house beside of the activity we completed.

Student: _____ Date: _____

Parent(s): _____ Date: _____

This page may be copied for student/parent use.

Jubilee Bike Race Heroes

Lesson #2   Chapters 4-6   Pages 45-85

Lesson Focus: Suhcrom, Naddih and their friends set out to find a way to raise money to help their friend.

Basic Story Vocabulary   (2-5, Reading – Standard 4)

deflated	spokes	frantically	bamboo
quivered	dumplings	worthy	aggressively
gangly	gully	unison	friction
commotion	jerk chicken	ration	bona fide
muffler	kerosene	canteen	braggadocious

Pre-teach vocabulary to introduce students to new words prior to reading the chapter. Choose an *Instructional Vocabulary Activity* from page 31.

Reading the Text

Silly Nomad books make fun read-aloud experiences for students. Varying these strategies reinforces interaction with text and creates ongoing interest for students. Choose a *Read-Aloud Strategy* from page 32-33 for in-class reading.

Facilitated Discussion Prompts

👀   Have you ever stepped in to help a friend who was being bullied or to stop a fight? Talk about what happened and why you decided to help? (2-5, Speaking & Listening – Standards 1, 4, & 6)

👀 What would you do if you broke something that you borrowed from a friend? Would you tell them you broke it? Would you offer to fix it? Share your thoughts with a small group. Does everyone agree with how each person would handle this situation? (2-5, Speaking & Listening – Standards 1, 2, & 6)

👀 With a partner, make a prediction about what you think will happen next. Will Suhcrom and Naddih get back to Palmerston Close in time to help fix Nigel's bike for the big race? Will Nigel be able to compete in the race at all? (2-5, Speaking & Listening – Standards 1, 2, & 6)

👀 What kinds of things should Nigel do to train for the big bike race? Together with a small group, come up with a training plan for Nigel. (2-5, Speaking & Listening – Standards 1, 2, & 6)

👀 If you were going to make a movie out of this book, which actors would you choose to play the main characters? Explain why you would pick those people to play each character? (2-5, Speaking & Listening – Standards 1, 2, & 6)

Reading Comprehension Activities

👀 Continue the timeline of words and pictures that you created in the first lesson. Retell 5 – 10 events of the chapters you just read, and add them to your timeline in the order in which they occurred. Add to your story map as you continue to read to the end of the book. (2-5, Reading – Standards 2 & 7)

👀 In chapter 5, Miss Paulette tells Rodney, Naddih, and Muffet that Nigel is very lucky. Why does she think that? Find 3-5 details in the story to support her statement. Write your answer in complete sentences. (2-5, Reading – Standards 2 & 4)

👀 Describe the relationship between Suhcrom, Naddih, and their friends. Be specific and give details from the story to support your reasons for the way you describe their relationship. (2-5, Reading – Standards 1, 4 & 8)

👀 Using a Venn diagram, compare and contrast Suhcrom and Naddih. What character traits do they both have? How are their personalities different? (2-5, Reading – Standards 2, 4, & 8)

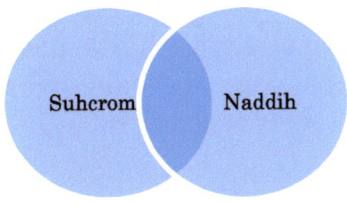

Writing Prompts

👀 💡 Imagine that you are going to compete in a race. Write and illustrate a story showing how you trained for the race and what happened on race day. Publish the story and share it with the class. (2-5, Writing – Standards 3, 5, & 6)

👀 Write and illustrate a story that starts with these sentences: *The area beyond the road sloped slightly downhill towards the swamp. The grass was damp and the almond trees rustled in the gentle sea breeze. Because of the slope of the land, we didn't see.....* Publish the story and share it with the class. (2-5, Writing – Standard 3 & 5)

👀 🎨 Imagine that you are visiting a junkyard. Write and illustrate a poem about your adventure at the junkyard. Your poem can be funny or scary. Share your poem with your class. (2-5, Writing – Standard 1; 2-5, Speaking & Listening – Standard 1, 3, & 6)

👀 🎨 Look at the illustration on page 59. Create your own characters and write your own story to go along with the illustration. (2-5, Writing – Standard 3 & 5)

Curriculum Connections

 **The Olympics**
Research your favorite Olympic athlete. Get an empty cereal box and wrap it in plain paper. Draw or find a photo of your athlete, place it on the front of the box and write at least 5 interesting facts along the side or back of the box. (2-5, Writing – Standards 1 & 7; 2-5, Reading – Standards 5 & 9)

 **Bottles and Cans**
The children collected bottles and cans to earn some money to pay for Nigel's bike to get fixed. If each bottle was worth 5 cents and each can was worth 2 cents, how much money would they earn if they collected 25 bottles and 15 cans? 36 bottles and 23 cans? Draw pictures or create equations to show how you solved the problems. (2-5, Writing – Standard 2)

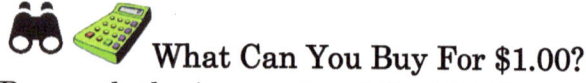 **What Can You Buy For $1.00?**
Research the internet and find 20 things that you can buy for $1.00. Print or draw a picture of each item and create a collage. Give your collage the same title as Chapter 4 in the book. Be sure to list where you found each item for $1.00. (2-5, Reading – Standard 5)

 **Different Foods**
Research some of the common foods that people eat in Jamaica and compare them to the foods eaten in your country. Use words and pictures to create a Venn diagram showing the similarities and differences between the foods of each country. (2-5, Reading – Standard 5)

Research & Imagination Activities

 **Imagine a business...**

Imagine you needed to earn some money for something. What would you do? Create a business plan for yourself and document it, either digitally or on paper so you can share it with your class. Include what you would do (ex: walk dogs), how often you would do it, how much you would charge, and what your end goal would be. Create a business card to go along with your plan. (2-5, Writing – Standards 1 & 2)

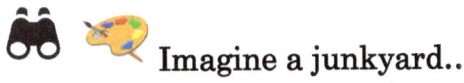 **Imagine a junkyard...**

Imagine you were at a junkyard. What kinds of things would you find there? Find pictures of 6 things that you would find in a junkyard and figure out how you would repurpose them or use them in another way. Glue your pictures on to a poster board and then explain how you would repurpose each item using pictures and words. (2-5, Writing – Standard 2)

 **Imagine a bike race...**

Imagine you are the organizer of a bike race around your city or town. Using a website like Google Earth or MapQuest, find a map of your city and determine what route the race will follow. Draw or print the map and highlight the race route. Explain why you chose the route that you did. (2-5, Writing – Standard 2)

Jubilee Bike Race Heroes - Volume 3

Lesson #2   Home Connection Activities

🏠 Research a typical Jamaican recipe. With a parent, create a shopping list and make the recipe. Using all five senses, write a diamante poem explaining the experience of cooking the food and eating it.

🏠 Research the types of things that you use at home, such as cans and bottles, that can be recycled. Ask a friend or relative to help you collect them for one week and see how much you can recycle together.

🏠 Draw and color a picture of your favorite scene from the story so far. Show your drawing to a parent and explain what is happening and why it is your favorite part of the story.

🏠 Go for a bike riding adventure with a sibling or a parent. Afterwards, talk about all the things that you saw and experienced while on your adventure. Draw a picture of your adventure.

WE CONNECTED!

My favorite character in this part of the story was _____

because he/she _____

I liked the part in the story when _____

_____

I circled the house beside of the activity we completed.

Student: _____ Date: _____

Parent(s): _____ Date: _____

This page may be copied for student/parent use.

Jubilee Bike Race Heroes

Lesson #3   Chapters 7-8   Pages 87-110

Lesson Focus: Suhcrom, Naddih and their friends cheer for Nigel as he competes in the Annual Jubilee Bike Race.

Basic Story Vocabulary   (2-5, Reading – Standard 4)

tar	cautious	aroma	jostled
reins	piercing	stubborn	handkerchief
competitor	reggae	festive	trinkets
overcome	thoroughbred	rallied	veered
jubilee	mansion	dribbling	salvage

Pre-teach vocabulary to introduce students to new words prior to reading the chapter. Choose an *Instructional Vocabulary Activity* from page 31.

Reading the Text

Silly Nomad books make fun read-aloud experiences for students. Varying these strategies reinforces interaction with text and creates ongoing interest for students. Choose a *Read-Aloud Strategy* from page 32-33 for in-class reading.

Facilitated Discussion Prompts

👓 Mr. Burke put a pirate flag on Nigel's bike. What do you know about pirates? Why do you think a pirate flag has a skull on it? Have a discussion with a partner about pirates. Were they usually good people or bad people? Why? (2-5, Speaking & Listening – Standards 1, 4, & 6)

👀 Watch a short video on YouTube about the Tour de France. Compare and contrast the race in the book with this race. (2-5, Speaking & Listening – Standards 1, 2, 4, & 6)

👀 Talk about your favorite part of the book with a friend. Tell why it is your favorite part. Then ask your friend what their favorite part is and why. Compare the two scenes and try to convince the other person to like your part better. (2-5, Speaking & Listening – Standards 1, 2, & 6)

👀 How would the story have been different if Mr. Wheeler had been driving a pickup truck instead of a donkey pulling a cart full of fruit? Discuss this with a friend. What would he have had in the back of the pickup truck instead? (2-5, Speaking & Listening – Standards 1, 2, & 6)

👀 One of the messages in this story is that each one of us is a hero in some way. What are some characteristics of a hero? What unique hero characteristics do you possess? Talk with a partner about a time you demonstrated being a hero. (2-5, Speaking & Listening – Standards 1, 2, & 6)

Reading Comprehension Activities

👀 Finish the timeline of words and pictures that you started in the first two lessons. Retell 5 – 10 events of the chapters you just read, and add them to your timeline in the order in which they occurred. (2-5, Reading – Standards 2 & 7)

👀 Onomatopoeia is when the author uses words to describe the sounds of the thing he/she is writing about. Find five examples of onomatopoeia in the story. Create a chart with the sounds and what the author is describing. (2-5, Reading – Standards 4 & 8)

Create a movie trailer for Jubilee Bike Race Heroes. You can use a program like Movie Maker or iMovie, or you can act it out. (2-5, Reading – Standards 2 & 3)

Using a paper doll shape, create a paper doll for two of your favorite characters in the story. Dress the paper doll the way you think the character would dress. Attach a sheet of paper to the back of the doll with the name of the character, a short description, tell why he/she is your favorite character, and how do you think the story would be different without them in it. (2-5, Reading – Standards 4 & 7)

Writing Prompts

Mr. Wheeler's donkey cart was full of different kinds of fruits. What is your favorite fruit? Using your five senses, describe the fruit and explain why it is your favorite. Be sure to use lots of descriptive words. (2-5, Writing – Standards 1 & 2)

Rewrite the last chapter from Nigel's point of view. How did he feel before, during and after the race? (2-5, Writing – Standard 3; 2-5, Reading – Standard 6)

Write a letter to a famous movie producer persuading them to make this book into a movie. Explain why you think that the story would make a good movie. (2-5, Writing – Standard 1, 2 & 5)

Imagine you were interviewing one of the characters in the book. Write out 10 questions that you would ask that character about what happened in the story and their role in it. Then answer the questions the way that you think the character would answer it. (2-5, Writing – Standard 1 & 3)

Curriculum Connections

 Take a Vacation

Research some interesting places to visit in Jamaica. Create a travel brochure with pictures and descriptions of these places, encouraging people to visit Jamaica on their next vacation. (2-5, Writing – Standards 1, 2 & 7; 2-5, Reading – Standards 5 & 7)

 Tour de France

The Tour de France is one of the most famous races for cyclists. Research the last Tour de France. Create a graph to show the distance of each leg of the race and as well as the winner of each leg. Add up all the distances to find the total number of miles that they ride during this race. (2-5, Reading – Standards 3 & 5)

 Play a Game

Design and make a board game to go along with the book. Use the characters and the setting in your game. Remember to include the rules of the game as well. Exchange your game with a friend and play. (2-5, Reading – Standard 5 & 7)

 Sun Protection

The sun has lots of benefits but too much sun can also be hazardous to your health. Research some ways that the sun can be damaging as well as ways that you can protect yourself from sunburns, heatstroke and other sun related issues. Create 3 paper dolls to represent 3 different ways that we can protect ourselves from getting too much sun. (2-5, Reading – Standard 5 & 8)

Research & Imagination Activities

Imagine a TV reporter…

Imagine you are a TV reporter and you have to do a report on the race that Nigel was competing in. Have a friend or adult record you as a reporter reporting "live" from the Jubilee Bike Race in Portsmouth, Jamaica. (2-5, Writing – Standards 2 & 3)

Imagine pirates…

Imagine you were a pirate. Many pirates had special flags with symbols that represented what they did or something about them. Research some famous pirates and their flags. Now design your own pirate flag with symbols to represent something about you. Use construction paper to create your flag and share it with the class. (2-5, Reading – Standards 1 & 7)

Imagine a trip to Jamaica…

Imagine you were going on a trip to Jamaica to visit Suhcrom and Naddih for a week. Research some places that you would like to go and the foods that you would like to try while you are there. Create a journal using words and pictures of your adventures with the boys and their friends. List each day as a separate journal entry and tell what you did, what you ate and who you were with. (2-5, Writing – Standards 3, 5 & 7)

Jubilee Bike Race Heroes - Volume 3

Lesson #3   Home Connection Activities

🏠 Research how to make a smoothie. With a parent, make a smoothie with your favorite fruit as the main ingredient. Then, discuss other ways that you could use the fruit and how you think it would taste (for example: ice cream, jam, or salad dressing).

🏠 Listen to a reggae song by Bob Marley. Now summarize what happened in the book and turn it into a reggae-style song. Sing your song for a parent or family member.

🏠 Using a milk carton or bottle, design a trophy for the winner of the Jubilee Bike Race. Paint it, or use other craft materials to decorate the trophy.

🏠 Using a coat hanger and string, create a mobil with pictures of important events that happened in the book.

WE CONNECTED!

My favorite character in this part of the story was _____

because he/she _____

I liked the part in the story when _____

_____

I circled the house beside of the activity we completed.

Student: _____ Date: _____

Parent(s): _____ Date: _____

This page may be copied for student/parent use.

Instructional Vocabulary Activities

(2-5, Reading – Standard 4)

Frayer Diagram: Divide the paper into fourths. Write a vocabulary word in the center (or the intersection of both lines). In one corner, place your own definition of the word. In the second corner, place facts or characteristics of the vocabulary word, and in the third, place examples of the word, and in the fourth, place non-examples of the word.
http://www.longwood.edu/staff/jonescd/projects/educ530/aboxley/graphicorg/fraym.htm

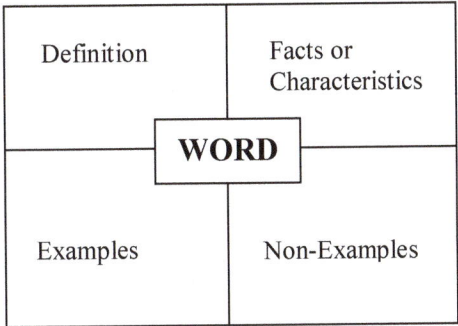

Word Sorts: Organize all of the vocabulary words into groupings that have common characteristics. Make up as many grouping titles as needed to go with the groupings. To vary the activity, sort the words by character association (which words are best associated with which story character), a great pre and post reading activity.

Add Words to an Interactive Word Wall: Include every new vocabulary word introduced on an interactive word wall. Interactive word walls are comprised of a wall or classroom space, wall, door, bulletin board, divider, etc. which is designated for these new words. Words are printed or created and then placed on the wall for frequent student use through discussion, writing, review, reading, grouping, illustration, or manipulation throughout classroom activities. The more the words are used following introduction, the more effective and interactive the Word Wall becomes for students.

Read-Aloud Strategies

(2-5, Speaking & Listening – Standards 1 & 2; 2-5, Reading – Standard 4)

Buddy Reading: Place students into pairs prior to reading. Students take turns reading out loud to each other, each a page or paragraph at a time.

Popcorn Reading (after Silent Pre-Reading): After an initial silent reading of the passage, one person begins to read the passage aloud. As soon as he/she stops reading, another student "pops" in to continue where the previous student stopped reading. It is helpful to set ground rules at the beginning of this activity, such as a maximum or minimum number of sentences or words read. This activity reinforces attention to print, listening, and collaboration as the object is to complete a passage in a smooth manner. It is important to allow the students to take the initiative to read rather than calling on them.

Jigsaw Reading: Jigsaw reading is helpful for use with longer passages or multiple passages of related text content. Split the passage(s) into sections and assign each section to a group of students so that every group reads a different part of the entire passage. The groups work together to read and understand their assigned passage. Their responsibility is to return to the whole group to summarize and/or teach them the content of their assigned passage. As a variation, allow the groups choices in how they teach the content to the entire group.

Choral Reading: Choral reading can be accomplished several different ways. It can include an initial silent read, and preplanning of how the passage can be most effectively read together. Choose parts of the passage to be read chorally, all students reading aloud together, and parts to be read aloud by one person or several different people. Commonly, the specific parts you want students to recall are those selected for choral reading. Choral reading can be fun as well as support and encourage listening skills and active engagement.

Read with Main Idea or Timeline Maps/Advanced Organizers: Main idea maps are a type of advanced organizer that effectively supports students in getting meaning from passages. A skeleton main idea map is most helpful in starting students with this strategy. Provide a web or diagram showing the main idea of the passage, as well as designated blank areas for the main points supporting the main idea that are connected to the main idea. Students read the passage aloud or silently and complete the map with the main points, as well as minor detail supporting those main points. This can be accomplished collectively out loud or as individuals in silence. In time, students can move to creating their own mind maps of passages. Use SmartArt in Microsoft Word for templates.

Oral Reading with CLOZE: For younger students, the teacher can read the book aloud to a group of students, periodically pausing for students to complete the appropriate word in text based on listening comprehension, syntax, and language skills.

Live Theatre Reading: After an initial reading of the passage, allow students to take different character roles within the story and read it as a play. The narrator reads any parts not in direct quotations. This interactive reading, especially when done in small groups, allows students to practice reading skills while they pay close attention to quotation marks, conversation between characters, and listening skills.

ASSESSMENTS

Pre and Post Assessments, Quizzes, and
Reading Comprehension Assessments
may be copied for student use.

Jubilee Bike Race Heroes - Volume 3
Pre and Post Assessment

Place T (truth) or M (myth) by each statement.

Pre	Statement	Post
	"Bike flying" means to race bicycles really fast.	
	Space Ghost is the name of a real cartoon superhero.	
	Jamaica is divided into 15 parishes.	
	People catch turtles for their meat.	
	In the movie, E.T., he gets on a skateboard and flies to the moon.	
	You have to wear goggles to protect you when you are going to ride a bike over a ramp.	
	Boys are always better at riding bikes than girls.	
	We should always stand up for people who can't stand up for themselves.	
	A hubcap makes a really good boomerang.	
	The best way to escape an alligator is to run in a zig-zag.	
	In Jamaica, they eat a lot of plantains.	
	You can't find anything good at a junkyard.	

Jubilee Bike Race Heroes - Volume 3
Pre and Post Assessment

Answer Key

Pre	Statement	Post
M	"Bike flying" means to race bicycles really fast.	
T	Space Ghost is the name of a real cartoon superhero.	
M	Jamaica is divided into 15 parishes.	
T	People catch turtles for their meat.	
M	In the movie, E.T., he gets on a skateboard and flies to the moon.	
M	You have to wear goggles to protect you when you are going to ride a bike over a ramp.	
M	Boys are always better at riding bikes than girls.	
T	We should always stand up for people who can't stand up for themselves.	
M	A hubcap makes a really good boomerang.	
M	The best way to escape an alligator is to run in a zig-zag.	
T	In Jamaica, they eat a lot of plantains.	
M	You can't find anything good at a junkyard.	

Jubilee Bike Race Heroes - Volume 3

Lesson #1 Quiz   Chapters 1-3

1. Why was Space Ghost Suhcrom's favorite cartoon?
   a. He had a cape.
   b. He could freeze and destroy his enemies.
   c. He could make wristbands from toilet paper rolls.

2. Where did Naddih find his watch?
   a. In the backyard
   b. In the couch
   c. In the swamp

3. Who was the first one to see the turtle that the fisherman caught?
   a. Mikal
   b. Rodney
   c. Sterlin

4. Why did the boys want to leave the house before Enomih woke up?
   a. She was mean to them.
   b. She would give them chores to do.
   c. She wouldn't let them go bike flying.

5. In Chapter 2, what caused Suhcrom to say, *"Yah mon, wi fool-fool eeh"*?
   a. They let the boat drift away.
   b. They wanted to see the turtle that the fisherman caught.
   c. They all jumped in the water because they thought there was a shark.

6. Which sentence explains why the boys were excited?
   a. The smell of fried eggs and dumplin' filled the air.
   b. They heard the chirp-chirp-chirping of the birds as they made their way toward the soccer field at the edge of town.
   c. They had all done bike flying in the street by their houses before, but never on the hill by the Hart Academy.

7. Why did Naddih think that Nigel's bike was cool?
   a. It was pretty.
   b. It had lots of cool gadgets.
   c. It was fast.

8. What does the word <u>relieved</u> mean in the following passage from page 43?

   > They all started cheering and clapping. Sterlin let out a huge bellow of air, <u>relieved</u> that his little brother was okay. He helped him up off the ground, got him his feet again, and brushed the dirt from his clothes.

   a. happy
   b. relaxed
   c. worried

9. What most likely was the reason why Rodney fell off the bike?
   a. He started from too high up on the hill.
   b. He ate too much plantain before he went bike flying.
   c. He didn't have any goggles to help him see.

10. What did Suhcrom mean when he said that Rodney had "nine lives"?
    a. He was nine years old.
    b. He could survive anything.
    c. He had ridden a bike nine times.

42

Jubilee Bike Race Heroes - Volume 3

Lesson #2 Quiz   Chapters 4-6

1. Why did Rodney feel dizzy when they were going to tell Nigel about his bike?
   a. He was still hurt from falling off the bike.
   b. He was scared that Nigel would be mad.
   c. He was hungry.

2. Choose the correct order of the sentences as they happened in the story.
   Sentence A: Their eyes lit up with excitement as they filled each of their crocus bags.
   Sentence B: Rodney let go of Sterlin and Naddih and darted towards the object, pointing as he ran.
   Sentence C: The boys dropped to the ground inside the fence, kicking up a cloud of dust around their ankles as they landed.

   a. A, B, C
   b. B, A, C
   c. C, B, A

3. Which sentence describes Nigel's feelings when he saw his bike?
   a. He glanced past them to where the bike lay on the ground and instantly saw the twisted handle bars.
   b. Usually, he was rather meek-mannered and didn't get upset at much of anything.
   c. His throat tightened as disappointment spread across his face.

4. Why did the children NOT want Rodney to hold on to the money for Mr. Burke?
   a. They were afraid he would use it to pay for Nigel's bike to be fixed.
   b. They were afraid he would use it to buy more food.
   c. They were afraid he would lose it.

5. In the flashback on pages 53-61, what did the boys buy with the dollar that Rodney found on the ground?
   a. Chicken wing
   b. Chicken leg
   c. Chicken neck

6. Why do you think Naddih needed a script when he was collecting bottles?
   a. He didn't want to forget what to say
   b. So he could blame Rodney for breaking Nigel's bike
   c. Because Muffet was very shy

7. Why did Miss Paulette think that Nigel was lucky?
   a. He had a nice bike
   b. His friends wanted to help him
   c. He won the race

8. Desreen was brave because
   a. She started the fight with the boy from the Box Juice Gang
   b. She was picking on Darius during recess
   c. She made Delroy apologize to Darius

9. Desreen and Naddih are alike because
   a. They both helped a friend
   b. They can both do wheelies on a bike
   c. They both like to tell stories

10. What did Naddih put in his pocket at the junk yard?
    a. A hubcap
    b. A reflector
    c. A pair of broken sunglasses

Jubilee Bike Race Heroes - Volume 3

Lesson #3 Quiz   Chapters 7-8

1. When Naddih says, *"Why him jus a falla wi so?"* who is he talking about?
   a. Mr. Wheeler
   b. The sun
   c. Suhcrom

2. Where was Mr. Wheeler going?
   a. Market
   b. Palmerston Close
   c. To visit Mama

3. What did Suhcrom and Naddih NOT find at the junkyard?
   a. Handlebars
   b. Hubcap
   c. Reflector

4. Why was Nigel's mother going to buy him the Jamaican Jet Street Racer Bike?
   a. She wanted him to enter the race
   b. She wanted him to join the Cadet Program
   c. She wanted him to overcome his fear of competitions

5. What does the word sea mean in the sentence below?

   Nigel took his place among the sea of boys and girls who were gathered at the starting line.

   a. There were a lot of boys and girls.
   b. The starting line was in the shape of the letter C.
   c. The starting line was in the ocean.

6. Why do the children think that Delroy is nothing but trouble?
   a. He was a surprise competitor in the race.
   b. He has a friend named Calvin.
   c. He stole the flag off of the bike in front of him.

7. What happened BEFORE Rodney threw water at Nigel?
   a. Nigel fell off of his bike.
   b. Delroy passed Nigel.
   c. Nigel was in second place.

8. Why did Naddih think they were like superheroes?
   a. It reminds him of *Superman and His Amazing Friends*
   b. They saved the world
   c. They helped Nigel win the race.

9. Which sentence helps you to understand that Nigel won the race?
   a. With every ounce of strength he had, he pushed with all of his might and inched past the two riders just as they crossed the line.
   b. Nigel finally freed himself from the tangle of the other bikers and pulled out ahead.
   c. He was neck and neck with Fletcher and Axel as they approached the finish line.

10. Read the passage below from the story and then answer the question.

    > They all stood silently. Their eyes widened as they watched Mr. Burke count out seven quarters, six dimes and eight nickels. "Kids, this is not the amount we agreed upon," he said kindly. "However, I will take this as full payment because you all took responsibility for breaking your friend's bike and have worked so hard to raise the money to fix it."

    What can you infer about Mr. Burke from this passage?

    a. He likes to count money
    b. He is proud of the children
    c. He was mad that they broke Nigel's bike

Silly Nomads Jubilee Bike Race Heroes – Volume 3

Quiz Answer Key

Question	Lesson 1 Quiz	Lesson 2 Quiz	Lesson 3 Quiz
1	B	B	B
2	A	B	A
3	A	C	A
4	B	B	C
5	C	C	A
6	C	A	C
7	B	B	B
8	A	C	C
9	A	A	A
10	B	B	B

Jubilee Bike Race Heroes – Volume 3

Reading Comprehension Assessment

1. Suhcrom told Naddih, "You're always saying *fool-fool* things…" Find 5 examples from the story to support Suhcrom's statement about Naddih.

2. What connections can you make with this story? Can you connect to it because something similar happened in your life? Can you connect it with another book that you have read? Describe the connection.

3. A lot of authors use fiction to teach a lesson. What do you think is the lesson that the author is trying to teach us in this story? Explain your thinking and use details from the story to support your answer.

4. Find 3 examples in the story of how the children worked together to solve a problem.

5. Compare and contrast the adventures of Suhcrom and Naddih and the types of adventures that you have as child. How does where you live make a difference to the type of adventures you might have. Imagine Suhcrom and Naddih lived in your town. How would that change the story?

Silly Nomads

Look for these other Silly Nomads adventures!

Volume 1 – Silly Nomads From Palmerston Close

Volume 2 – Silly Nomads Go Ninja Crazy

Volume 4 – Coming Soon